NORTH AMERICAN INDIAN MASKS

◆

CRAFT AND LEGEND

◆

BY FRIEDA GATES

WALKER AND COMPANY NEW YORK, NEW YORK

Library of Congress Cataloging in Publication Data

Gates, Frieda.
    North American Indian masks.
    Summary: Describes masks used by North American
Indians to heal sickness, appease spirits, pray for
rain, and for other purposes.
    Includes directions for making several types of masks.
    1. Indians of North America—Masks—Juvenile
literature.   2. Indians of North America—Legends.
[1. Indians of North America—Masks.   2. Masks.
3. Handicraft]   I. Title.
E98.M3G37   1982   731'.75   82-2640
ISBN 0-8027-6462-2   AACR2
ISBN 0-8027-6463-0 (lib. bdg)

Photographs on pages 8, 9, and 10 are from the mask collec-
tion of Ivan Till. Photographs on pages 17, 18, 29, 32, 38, and
39, courtesy of the American Museum of Natural History.

First published in the United States of America in 1982 by the
Walker Publishing Company, Inc.

Published simultaneously in Canada by John Wiley & Sons
Canada, Limited, Rexdale, Ontario.

ISBN: 0-8027-6462-2 Trade
       0-8027-6463-0 Reinf.

Library of Congress Catalog Card Number: 82-2640

Printed in the United States of America

10 9 8 7 6 5 4 3 2 1

CONTENTS

INTRODUCTION

The Indians of North America believed that spirits influenced their lives and were responsible for everything important: the weather, their food supply, and even their well-being. To appease these spirits or "gods," they performed rituals. Certain members of the tribes wore masks during these ceremonies. The masks were made of wood, animal hides, shells, gourds, or other materials, depending on where the Indians lived. Some masks were intricately carved, some were elaborately decorated, and others were crudely made.

The Mandan Indians of North Dakota wore masks made from the heads of dead animals. The Indians that lived in Tennessee made masks by carving large white seashells. The most intriguing masks, however, were made by four diverse groups of Indians: the Iroquois of the eastern woodlands, the Pueblo Indians of the Southwest, the Indians who lived on the northwest coast, and the Eskimos of Alaska. Although these groups were separated by many miles and had very different life-styles, they each made masks that represented the spirits they worshipped. Religious beliefs and legends played an important role in the creation, design, and care of their masks. The Iroquois, Eskimo, and Northwest Coast Indians carved their masks of wood. In the Southwest, where trees were scarce, masks were made mostly from hides. Some birds were regarded as messengers of the gods, and their feathers were often used for decoration.

Only certain members in each group were allowed to make or wear masks. The men who wore them believed that they had the power to commune with the spirits. Some even believed they wore the mask of a particular spirit and therefore possessed its power.

Facsimiles of these masks can be made from easily obtained materials. The masks can be worn or used as decoration. Instructions provide details for reproduction of old masks and also for the creation of new adaptations and designs. Easy instructions are also included for masks that can be made quickly.

EASTERN IROQUOIS FALSE FACES

False Face Society members shake turtle-shell rattles and bang sticks together during their dances. This Seneca mask is black with a bifunnelate-blower mouth and a protruding tongue.

The Iroquois nation consisted of six tribes—the Mohawk, Oneida, Onondaga, Cayuga, Seneca, and Tuscarora—living in the area from Lake Erie to the Hudson River in New York State. The Iroquois suffered from many of the same ailments common today, such as colds, upset stomachs, headaches, and toothaches. They also suffered from accidents resulting in broken bones, sprained muscles, cuts, and burns. Eight to ten Iroquois families lived together inside a long, narrow house, and each family had its own area. The crowding together—especially in winter—caused illnesses to spread quickly from one family to another. Because fresh food was scarce, their diets were poor. Squash was their only fresh winter vegetable, and often they did not have meat.

During the summer the old women of the tribe gathered herbs, roots, and bark and concocted them into a variety of medicines. They also made salves from bear fat and bandages from corn husks. They used these medicines to help ease the suffering of sickness.

The Iroquois believed that all diseases were caused by evil spirits, so if the old women could not find a cure, the patient had to ask the False Face Society for help. Every village had a False Face Society. No one knew who the members were except the members themselves. They were all men, except for one or two older women who took care of the masks.

In order for a man to become a member of the False Face Society, he had to have been cured by it, or he had to have had a dream in which a spirit summoned him. In the dream the spirit told him how to make a mask that would give him healing powers, and it taught him a healing song. The next morning he went in secret to the old woman who kept the masks and told her about his dream. The old woman arranged a meeting of the society members where he repeated his dream so the members could interpret it and consider whether he could join their society.

Sometimes several days passed before the man received a sign that he was accepted. Then one morning he might find two tiny masks hanging on his doorpost. The masks were about three inches long and had large noses, twisted mouths, and long tufts of hair attached to each side. A small sack containing a few grains of tobacco hung from the masks. Now that he was accepted, the next step was to make his mask, so he went into the woods to find a proper tree. The mask had to be cut from a living tree that was full of sap. Basswood was most often used, but willow or other soft woods were also acceptable. After he selected a tree, he visited it once a day for a period of three days. Each time he came, he burned tobacco close to the tree as an offering. He also blew smoke from his pipe among the branches and over the roots. He had to ask forgiveness from the tree for having to cut into it.

After the three-day ceremony, he stripped off part of the bark and carved a rough outline of the mask into the living tree. Then he cut the portion containing the mask from the trunk. He took the partially carved mask home to be completed according to the instructions he had received in his dream. After the details of the mask were completed, he polished it. If the tree from which the mask was carved had been chosen in the morning, he colored the mask red by rubbing it with red ocher. If the tree had been chosen in the afternoon, he colored it black with charcoal. Next, he applied grease to make it smooth and shiny. Sometimes tin or copper rims were placed around the eyes.

The mask had to have special care. If the owner did not treat it properly, it would turn against him and give him the illnesses he tried to cure. When it wasn't being worn, the mask had to be hidden, face down, and covered. The Iroquois believed that if it were left in any other position, the mask and its powers would die. In order to please the spirit of the mask, the owner had to rub the lips occasionally with fat, and he had to offer it pinches of tobacco and cornmeal mush.

The new member of the False Face Society had to spend many hours learning the rituals and songs of the society. Because the masks hid only their faces, the Indians had to have costumes that would help conceal their identities. Some covered their bodies with old blankets; others stuffed bundles of skins or old rags under their shirts so they would look deformed. They made rattles from snapping-turtle shells,

7

Seneca red, crooked mouth

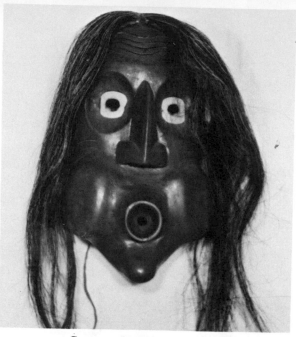

Cayuga red, whistling mouth

gourds, horn, or hickory bark. They also carried stout sticks.

The False Face Society members went from one longhouse to another driving away evil spirits and the illnesses they caused. When the False Faces arrived at the door of a longhouse, they shook their rattles and cracked their sticks together. They also chanted loud sounds like "hu, hu," and "han, han." The noises were made to announce their arrival as well as to scare the evil spirits.

The people of the house sat on benches or bunks along the walls. The False Faces entered in single file, stepping and shaking their rattles in rhythm. One of the members put out the fire so they could scoop up the ashes with their hands. Then they circled the room, sprinkling ashes over the heads of all the people while they shook their rattles and chanted. When they had sprinkled everyone with ashes,

one of the members built a new fire. After the fire started burning, it was time to treat the ailing person. Certain members of the society were thought to be successful at healing particular ailments, so the appropriate member then took charge and directed the other members. He usually rubbed ashes into the patient's scalp, blew upon it two or three times, sang a healing song, and led the dancing and singing of the group. Sometimes even the patient joined in. Dancing and singing were supposed to please the evil spirits, who would then leave the longhouse.

The people paid the society with offerings of tobacco and food.

When a man no longer wished to be a member of the society, he resigned in very much the same way he joined. He would dream that he was no longer a member and would relate the dream to the society.

Seneca light red-brown, smiling mouth

Mohawk dark red-brown, modified-distended
(variant spoon mouth)

LEGEND OF THE FALSE FACES

After the Great Spirit finished making the world, he walked all around the earth to rid it of evil spirits. When he came to the rim of the earth, he met a stranger. The Great Spirit asked the stranger what he was doing on his newly made earth. The stranger replied that it was *his* earth since he had been living on it from the time it was made. They argued until they finally agreed to settle the dispute by a contest. Whichever of them could successfully command a mountain to come to him would be able to command the world best.

The stranger shook his turtle-shell rattle and summoned a distant mountain to move toward him. The mountain slowly moved in his direction, and the stranger, pleased with his success, turned to the Great Spirit. The Great Spirit then commanded the mountain to stand next to the stranger. The mountain moved so quickly that the stranger turned his head to see what was happening. His face smashed into the side of the mountain, and the impact broke his nose and twisted his mouth in pain.

However, since the stranger did have power, the Great Spirit gave him the responsibilities of driving diseases from the earth and of aiding travelers and hunters. The stranger accepted the tasks on the condition that men would carve portrait masks of him, call him Grandfather, and make offerings of tobacco and cornmeal mush in his name.

9

Mohawk dark red-brown, spoon-mouth blower

Onondaga black, protruding tongue

FALSE FACES—SHAPES, COLORS, AND FEATURES

False Faces are oval masks, approximately 7 inches (18 cm) wide and 10 inches (25 cm) long. Some are larger. They have twisted and exaggerated features with many wrinkles. Although they are always painted red or black, the shades vary from light and dark reddish brown to bright red, and from gray to a deep black.

EYES Eyes are round, oval, or slanted (upward or downward). Eye holes are often surrounded with metal or bone. Holes are cut so the wearer can see.

NOSE Although not always broken—like that of the original spirit—noses are always large and protruding. Breathing holes are cut out of the nostrils.

MOUTH Often the most distinguishing feature, the mouth may be smiling, crooked, hanging, whistling, oval, distended, modified-distended, straight-distended, or skewed. Other mouth features include a protruding tongue, a square-mouth blower, a bi-funnelate blower, or a spoon-mouth blower. A hole is always made in the mouth.

HAIR Most masks have long horsehair attached at the top, which hangs loose or is braided. Sometimes they are decorated with fur or corn husks.

EARS False Faces do not have ears.

10

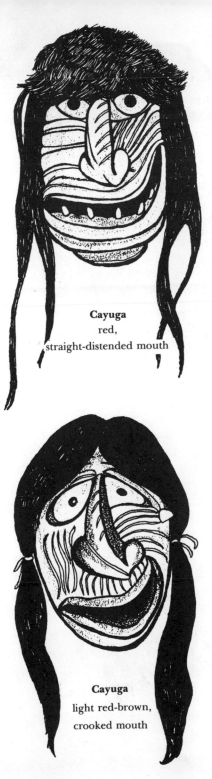

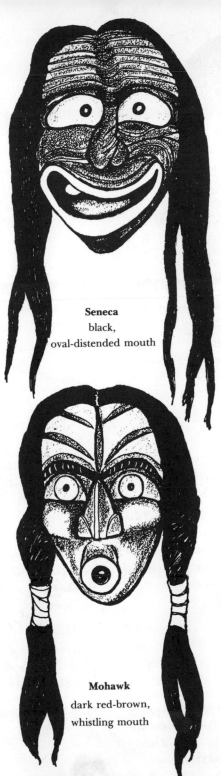

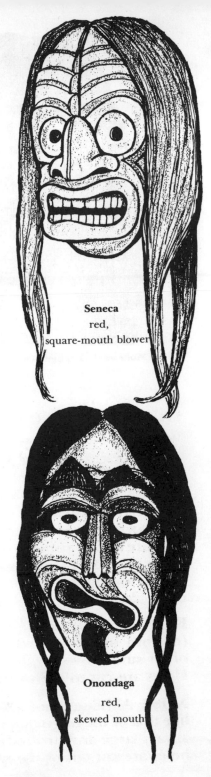

Cayuga
red,
straight-distended mouth

Seneca
black,
oval-distended mouth

Seneca
red,
square-mouth blower

Cayuga
light red-brown,
crooked mouth

Mohawk
dark red-brown,
whistling mouth

Onondaga
red,
skewed mouth

HOW TO MAKE A FALSE FACE-STYLE MASK

Since carving a mask out of wood presents many difficulties, a more convenient method is to use one of the following procedures. Copy one of the masks illustrated, or create your own. Always allow masks to dry before cutting or painting them. Cut holes for eyes, nostrils, and mouth. Paint with acrylics or poster paints. Surround eye holes with aluminum foil or shapes cut from aluminum pie plates. Other kinds of foil may also be bought in a craft store. Tops of frozen-juice cans are the right size. Hammer a large nail through the center in several places to make eye holes large enough to see through. Glue foil or can top onto mask. Hair can be made from lambswool*, yarn, or untwisted twine. Real or crepe-paper feathers** can be tied into the hair.

*Lambswool can be purchased wherever foot-care products are sold.
**Feather information follows mask methods.

DIRECTIONS AND RECIPES

Papier-mâché paste: Combine flour (non-self-rising), or library paste, or cornstarch, with enough water to make a creamy mixture.

Papier-mâché pulp: Combine thinned papier-mâché paste (above), or white glue, with shredded paper napkins, tissues, or toilet paper. Pulp can be molded like clay.

MOLD METHOD: Materials: modeling clay; papier-mâché paste; bowl, 6 inches in diameter, 3 inches deep (15 cm., 7 cm.); plastic wrap; Vaseline; and torn newspaper strips about 1 inch wide (3 cm.) soaked in water.

1. Turn bowl upside down and cover with plastic wrap.
2. Cover with clay and make mask shape. Add features.
3. Cover clay mold with newspaper strips, squeezed of excess water and dipped in paste.

Do not remove mask from mold before it is dry.

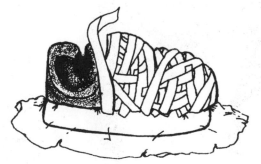

NO-MOLD METHOD: Materials: several sheets of newspaper; torn newspaper strips, about 1 inch wide (3 cm.), soaked in water; tape; and papier-mâché paste.

1. Roll two or three sheets of newspaper into a long tube about 28 inches (70 cm.) long. Use tape to hold it together.
2. Shape tube to fit around your face, and tape the overlapping ends. This is the mask frame.
3. Crush newspapers into a ball that will fit inside frame.
4. Cover newspaper ball with two sheets of newspaper. Tuck and tape sheets to inside edge of frame. Crushed newspaper ball should now be removable.
5. Build features with newspaper strips, squeezed of excess water and dipped into papier-mâché paste. Strips made into wads can be shaped into features. Make wrinkles from tightly rolled strips. Attach features and wrinkles with more dipped strips.

Note: Papier-mâché pulp can be used to shape features.

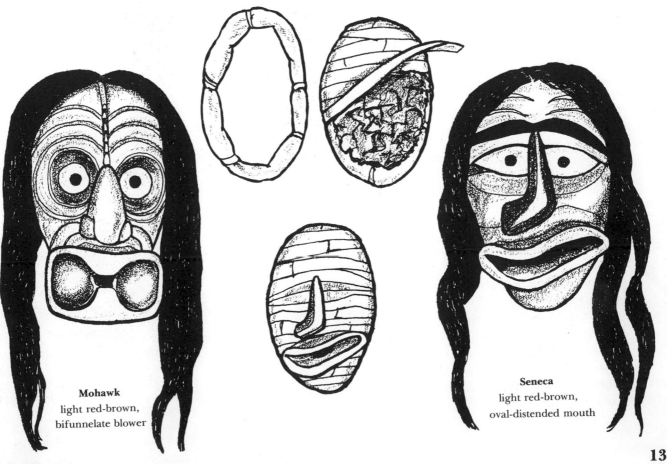

Mohawk
light red-brown,
bifunnelate blower

Seneca
light red-brown,
oval-distended mouth

CLOTH MÂCHÉ: A lighter-weight mask. Follow instructions for mold method, but use strips of cloth dipped into white glue thinned with water. Use cloth or paper wads to shape features.

GAUZE MÂCHÉ: Also a lightweight mask. This method makes two masks at one time. Gauze can be purchased in supermarkets or drugstores. Materials: papier-mâché paste or thinned white glue; blown-up balloon (size of your head or slightly larger); scissors; large empty can; wadded newspaper or papier-mâché pulp.

1. Rest balloon on can to hold it steady. Coat balloon with paste or glue.
2. Cover with three layers of gauze, using paste or glue between layers.
3. Create features for one or two masks (one on each side of balloon). Use wadded newspaper or papier-mâché pulp. Twisted strips of gauze will create wrinkles. Attach with gauze strips dipped in paste or glue.

Miniature False Faces are sometimes hung on a mask. They can be made by covering a ball of aluminum foil with any of the mâché methods including papier-mâché pulp. Miniatures can also be carved from balsa wood purchased in craft stores.

Seneca

light red-brown,
smiling mouth

Seneca

black,
hanging mouth

14

EASY MASK: Materials: cardboard (from shirts or boxes) 8 inches wide, 12 inches long (20 cm., 30 cm.); pencil; scissors; bowl of warm water; 1½-gallon bleach bottle (or something similar); wadded paper; tape; and string.

1. Draw and cut a large mask shape out of cardboard.
2. Soak cardboard mask in warm water until it is soft.
3. Create features by taping wadded paper shapes onto bottle.
4. Wrap and press wet cardboard mask to impress features into the mask. Tie mask on bottle.

   When dry, attach strips of paper or yarn for hair. Tie a string through a hole on each side to hold the mask on your head.

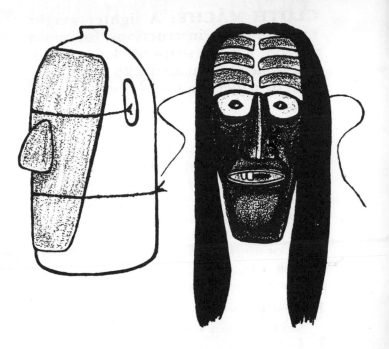

DIRECTIONS FOR MAKING CREPE-PAPER FEATHERS

Turkey, swan, or goose feathers can be purchased from a millinery or craft store. Some feathers may be found in parks. If real feathers are not available, make facsimiles from crepe paper and cotton. Use the following instructions for crepe-paper feathers.

Materials: white crepe-paper roll; absorbent cotton; pencil; scissors; tape; black felt-tip marker.

1. Cut one rectangle 12 inches by 4 inches (30 cm., 10 cm.) for each feather desired.
2. Fold rectangles in half lengthwise. Cut pointed feather shape halfway down each rectangle.
3. Gather base and wrap with tape. Cut slashes along edge of each side. Color tip with black marker.
4. Tufts: gather small wad of cotton at one end. Fan and fluff out the other end. Tape tuft to base of feather.

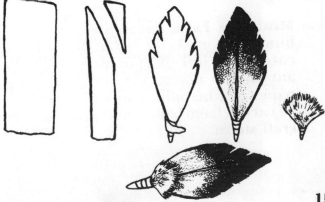

15

SOUTHWEST KACHINA MASKS

The Indians of the Southwest lived in New Mexico, Arizona, southern Colorado, Utah, western Texas, and northwestern Mexico. Many of the Southwest Indians lived in villages called "pueblos" and are referred to as Pueblo Indians. Among the Pueblo Indians are the Hopi of northwest Arizona, the Zuni of New Mexico, and the Acoma, who lived along the Rio Grande in New Mexico. The Navaho and Apache are also Southwest Indians.

Much of the land in this area is desert or semi-desert, and the climate is hot and dry. When there wasn't enough rain, crops would dry up, grass wouldn't grow, sheep—and even people—would die of thirst. Although these Indians worshipped many gods, they believed Mother Earth and Father Sky to be responsible for the weather and the crops. They communicated with these gods through spirits they called *kachinas*. Each kachina had a name, a distinctive appearance, and a particular duty or power. Over two hundred kachinas were identifiable, even by young Indian children.

Legends vary from one village to another, but kachina tales are basically the same. Long ago the little kachinas lived among the Indians and taught them how to fish and hunt, and how to make things useful and good to look at. When crops were dry, the kachinas per-

The Hopi *Hemis Kachina* is the principal character in the Niman dance. Held in July, it is the last kachina dance of the year. His helmet is half pink, half green; tableta has fertility and cloud symbols painted in directional colors. He wears a ruff of fir branches.

Kachina dolls of the Hopi Indians.

formed rituals to make it rain. But a quarrel between the Indian men and the kachinas caused the kachinas to leave. According to the Zuni legend, they went to live at the bottom of a lake in the empty desert. The Hopi say they went to live in the snow and ice of the San Francisco peaks near Flagstaff, Arizona. And still another legend says that the kachinas were massacred. In all the tales, however, the kachinas left behind their rawhide masks. The Indian men put on the masks, which were made in the image of the kachinas. When wearing the masks, they believed that the kachinas entered into them and gave them their spiritual powers.

Among the Apache and Navaho Indians, only the medicine men made and wore masks, but all Hopi and Zuni men were allowed to wear masks.

When Indian children watched the masked kachinas perform at ceremonies, they believed the kachinas were real spirits. Children were given dolls representing the many kachinas, and in this way they learned the kachina names and what they stood for. When a boy reached age twelve or thirteen, his parents took him to a kiva. A kiva is an underground circular chamber used for ceremonies by members of a kachina cult. Each Pueblo village had at least one kachina cult, and some villages had as many as six. Every man belonged to at least one cult.

In the kiva the boy would be surrounded by masked kachinas. The boy's father or an elder would explain to him the importance of the kachinas for the community. Then the kachinas whipped the boy with yucca leaves. The whipping wasn't painful, but it was very frightening because the boy still thought the kachinas were real spirits. After the whipping, the kachinas removed their masks to show the boy that they were only men. When the boy recognized them, they told him the legend of the kachinas. Next, the boy was allowed to whip the kachinas. He hit each one four times on each arm and each leg. Before leaving the kiva, the boy was instructed never to tell the younger children the

Sio Salako Green helmet, with black-and-white band across his eyes.

Malo Helmet is half green, half red. Blossom on one side of his head, red hair tuft and feathers on the other.

secret of the masked kachinas. For, if he did, he was told that the real kachinas would cut off his head and kick it all the way to the Sacred Lake, where they lived. After this initiation the boy was regarded as an adult and was allowed to participate in the ceremonies. Women were initiated into a cult only if they had been cured by a kachina ritual or if they mistakenly entered a kiva during a ceremony. However, girls were told the kachina secret when they came of age.

Members of a cult had to make their own masks. The Hopi and Zuni made their masks secretly, under the direction of kachina priests. A man inherited the right to be a priest, and he was regarded as a chief of the spirit world. It was his duty to give directions for the construction of masks and costumes, and instructions for the ceremonial rituals. Kachina masks often had to be repainted or replaced after a ceremony so that they would always be in perfect condition. Masks of the Apache and Navaho medicine men resembled those worn by the Pueblos in color and shape. They

wore their masks until they were worn out or until their magic disappeared. Since masks were sacred, they had to be treated carefully even when they were not in use. The masks were fed by being sprinkled with cornmeal and pollen to renew their powers.

Kachina ceremonies were performed each year for six months, beginning in December. During this time the kachina spirits were believed to be actually present. The masked kachinas took their responsibility very seriously. Each ceremony had a special purpose, but most of them involved asking for rain. If it did not rain, the Indians believed it was because they had done something wrong. Perhaps a design or color on a mask wasn't right, or a feather may have been out of place. It could have been an error in a costume or a dance. They believed that if a masked dancer was not pure of heart and did not believe intensely, he would be punished by the real kachina he was impersonating. As an Indian man put on his mask, he prayed to the kachina spirit not to cause him trouble.

KACHINA MASKS—SHAPES, COLORS, AND FEATURES

The helmet shapes are the most characteristic of the kachina masks. They are made by sewing together a cylindrical base and a circular top of rawhide. Other types include circular masks, made by stretching cloth over yucca-sifter baskets; full or half-face leather masks; and sack masks.

Colors and designs painted on masks are symbolic. Pueblo Indians associated colors with directions, so the color of a mask indicates where the kachina comes from. Yellow means the kachina comes from the north; blue-green from the west; red from the south; white from the east; black from below the earth; and all colors together from the sky. Design symbols are often painted on the forehead or the cheeks of a mask and are important distinguishing marks.

KACHINA MASK SYMBOLS

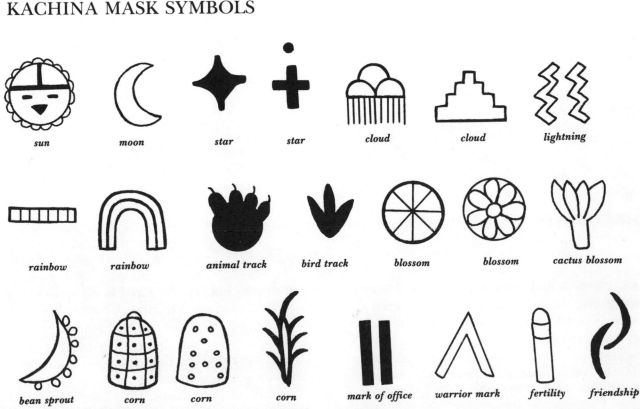

sun   moon   star   star   cloud   cloud   lightning

rainbow   rainbow   animal track   bird track   blossom   blossom   cactus blossom

bean sprout   corn   corn   corn   mark of office   warrior mark   fertility   friendship

EYES

Eye holes are small circular holes or narrow slits. They don't necessarily have to be the painted shapes or pop eyes of the mask face. Painted eyes may be rectangular (a), round (b), crescent-shaped (c), joined (d), pot-hooks (e), diagonals (f), or unmatched (g).

NOSES, MOUTHS, AND SNOUTS

Realistic noses are seldom seen. Breathing holes need not have any relation to the nose or mouth of the mask. Painted mouths may be round, rectangular, triangular, crescent-shaped, or formed by long lines with teeth across the front. A beak, tube, or snout* is often attached to the mask.

BEARDS*

These are made of horsehair or feathers or both. They are always attached to half-face masks.

EARS AND HORNS*

Usually these are made from the same material as the mask. Gourds, stuffed cloth, and real animal horns are also used.

HEADDRESSES

Feathers*, hair, wool, or wooden tabletas* adorn the tops of many masks.

RUFF*

This is used to hide the joining of the mask to the body. It is made of fir or juniper branches, fox skins, rags, or a cloth roll.

*Asterisks indicate directions—also substitutions that follow directions.

Avachoya (a) Helmet, any directional color with white surrounding eyes. Tube snout.

Mastof (b) Helmet, black with white designs. Grass ruff.

Chakwaina (c) Full face, black with red tongue. Hair beard, woolly lamb wig.

Sip-ikne (d) Helmet, any directional color with painted flower ears. Tube snout, feather ruff.

Mashanta (e) Green Helmet with cloud symbols.

Heheya-aumutaqa (f) Helmet, white with red designs. Branch ruff.

Hishab (g) Helmet, green with white spots. Tube snout, tufts of red hair on each side.

Angwusnasomtaqa Green helmet with black wings. Fur ruff.

Tukwunag White helmet. Tableta of cloud symbols with feathers hanging over the face. Branch ruff.

Sikya-chantaka Helmet, green with red outlining black-and-white band. Pop eyes, red ears, and snout.

Sivu-i-qiltaqa Helmet, black with red outlining white hand. Fur ruff.

Salako Helmet, white with red mouth. Tableta in all directional colors.

tableta   *front*   *back*

HOW TO MAKE A KACHINA-STYLE MASK

HELMET MASK This mask can be made from a 5-gallon (20-liter) cardboard ice cream container. Color the container with poster or acrylic paints. Cut out eyes and holes for breathing. Breathing holes do not need to be in the nose or mouth. Helmets can also be made from a large, cylindrical oatmeal container or a large plastic bleach bottle. Cut off the top and cut up the back of the oatmeal container or bottle. Remove labels. Color it with poster or acrylic paints. Poster board that is trimmed, rolled, and stapled into a cylinder to fit around your head may also be used.

CIRCULAR MASK Blow up a head-size balloon. Place it in a large juice can to hold it steady while you cover it with white glue or papier-mâché paste. (See page 12.) Layer gauze or strips of newspaper over the balloon. Use about three layers. Let dry for a day or more. Cut this hardened covering in half and make two masks.

FULL- OR HALF-FACE MASKS Make these from poster board or felt. Half masks have beards of hair or feathers attached to them. Use yarn, unraveled twine, felt or crepe-paper fringe, real or paper feathers. Tape, sew, or glue beard onto mask.

SACK MASKS Use an old pillowcase, or make a hood by sewing two pieces of felt (or other cloth) together to fit over your head. A pillowcase or a hood can be dyed or painted.

Eototo—Chief White helmet, branch ruff.

Wupomo Circular. *Top*, half yellow, half green; *bottom*, black. Long bill with hanging tongue. Fur ruff.

Hapota Full face, pink with carved wood nose.

Tasaf Anya Half face, green with yellow cheeks. Beard.

Toson Koyemsi—Mud Head Sack, brown with green designs. Short tube eyes and mouth.

22

Kwa—Eagle Helmet, green with black designs and yellow beak. Fur ruff.

Kwikwilyaqa Helmet, brown with white designs. Tube eyes and snout. Cloth ruff.

Fox Helmet, yellow with black-and-white designs.

Pachavuin Mana Orange half face with beard.

Kachin-mana Half face, yellow with black lines and eyes. Feather beard and red wig.

Poli—Butterfly Full face, blue with black features. Black wig.

Tawa—Sun Circular, green with red-and-yellow forehead. Surrounded with eagle feathers.

Hano—Clown Sack, black and white. Stuffed cloth horns, rag ruff.

Tata-nga-ya—Hornet Sack, multi-colored stripes. Long bill.

23

MASK FEATURES—DIRECTIONS AND SUBSTITUTIONS

Tutumsi Green helmet. Pop eyes and beard.

POP EYES Roll poster board, or use cardboard tubes from paper towels or toilet tissue. On paper draw and cut out two pieces of the shape shown. Cut solid lines and fold broken lines. Fold and insert tabs at ends of tubes.

SNOUTS Small empty food packages can be painted or covered with paper and inserted into slits in mask. Or follow pattern shown. Use heavy paper or poster board. Cut solid lines and fold broken lines. Glue A over B. Fold in flaps 1 and 2. Fold and glue flap C over D. Insert tabs and tape inside mask slits.

BEARDS Use unraveled twine or lambswool, colored red or black with dye, ink, or paint. Or use yarn, fringed crepe paper, or felt. Feather beards can be made out of cut paper, crepe paper, or real feathers.

HORNS Cut shapes from poster board, shirt cardboard, or corrugated cardboard. Paper-towel tubes, molded papier-mâché pulp, gourds, or a pair of stuffed baby's tights can be used.

Pahi-ala Helmet, white with black design. Pop eyes, snout, three horns, and branch ruff.

RUFF Use green crepe paper 6 inches (15 cm.) wide, and as long as paper will allow. Sew a running stitch lengthwise through the middle. Pull ruffle together to fit around the bottom of the mask. Or attach fringed rags or a stocking that is stuffed and painted with poster or acrylic paints. Glue, staple, or sew onto mask.

HEADDRESS Make from real or crepe-paper feathers (page 15), twine, or lambswool. Tabletas can be made from corrugated or shirt cardboard, poster board, tongue depressors, or Popsicle sticks.

Miniature Kachina Masks can be made using cardboard tubes from paper towels or toilet tissue.

Muzribi helmet, green with black design. Red tube snout and branch ruff.

Tukwinag—Cumulus Cloud Helmet, half white, half brown. Tableta with cloud symbols.

Hututu—Rain Priest Helmet, White with black. Wool wig and cloth ruff.

25

NORTHWEST COAST INDIAN MASKS

The Northwest Coast Indians lived in an area rich in resources from the ocean and forests. The region included the southeast coast of Alaska from Yakutat Bay southward, through British Columbia to the Columbia River County in Washington and Oregon. Indian groups from this area include the Tlingit, Haida, Tsimshian, Bella Coola, Kwakiutl, Nootka and Coast Salish peoples. These groups were divided into tribes that were made up of clans.

Clans were related through common ancestors, but not necessarily *human* ancestors. Clan legends claimed gods and supernatural beings—real and mythical—as heroic ancestors. Family crests representing ancestors were painted on the fronts of houses and carved into totem poles and masks. "To-tem" comes from the word "otoman" which means "his brother and sister kin." The designs carved on these tall wooden posts tell the story of a clan's history. Sometimes they commemorate an important event.

Masks were the most valued possessions of these people. Theirs were the most elaborate and intricately designed of all North American Indian masks. Although thousands of masks survive, never has anyone found two that are alike. Masks were worn for social and religious ceremonies, for secret society rituals, for healing the sick and driving away the causes of disease, and also for fun. Since these tribes had no written language to record their myths and legends, masks served as their history books.

These Indians of the Northwest believed that all things and all creatures possessed spirits. Their legends say that when the world began, these spirits and creatures could change from one form to another and speak a common language. Dangerous humanlike spirits and ghosts dwelt under the earth; powerful monsters under the sea; and giant birds in the sky, guarding the sun. To appease these spirits, the Indians lived by rigid rules.

A clan's masks representing a mythological ancestor was inherited and could only be worn by the owner. Potlatch ceremonies, in which an individual gave away his possessions, were special celebrations where clan masks were worn.

Masks were also worn by shamans, who were the vilage priests and doctors. A shaman wore a mask during healing rituals and ceremonies in which he talked with the spirits. Shamans usually carved their own masks, and each shaman had several. Secret society members wore masks for a variety of occasions, including initiation ceremonies, when a young person would be welcomed into the group.

Clan masks and secret society masks were carved by expert carvers and then painted. The right to be a mask carver had to be inherited, and an apprentice spent many years learning his craft. A chief or a high-ranking tribe member employed a carver to make his masks. The carver worked in secret so that a

faces hidden behind an outer face. Such masks required tremendous skill to construct and to operate. Some measured six feet long and weighed as much as forty pounds (18 kilo.).

Ceremonies were very dramatic productions that used all sorts of stage effects. They were performed at night by firelight. At the right moment, masked spirits rushed into the house screaming and dancing wildly. Small figures—actually puppets on strings—flew through the air. Ghostly voices seemed to come from the rafters, the fire, and from beneath the spectators. (In fact, unseen hollow kelp-stem tubes carried the sounds.) Stooges pretended to be possessed. Blood squirted from a filled animal bladder hidden under a dancer's costume. Trapdoors opened, and masked dancers rose from under the floorboards. Sometimes a masked

mask would not be seen until it was ready to be used. He carved the mask of cedar or alder wood that was still green and filled with sap, and painted it with colors he made from natural materials: vegetation, blood, fungus, bear dung, and rocks. He made some masks in parts that fastened together. He made some with small faces or figures surrounding a face. He even made masks with movable parts so that the mouth, neck, or eyes could open and close when the mask was worn. And he made transformation masks that had one or more

The evil bird spirit, Hoxhox, participates in the Kwakiutl Hamatsa ceremony. The Hamatsa or Cannibal Dance is an annual secret society ritual.

Performer opens and closes Hoxhox's beak.

Kwakiutl masks

demon bit one of the onlookers on an arm or leg. Dancers transformed their masks with the pull of a string. A wolf mask might become a bird. Drumming and rattles increased the din. Finally the shaman exorcised the masked demons and the evil spirits and, after a while, calmed the tribe members.

SHAPES, COLORS, AND FEATURES

The masks worn in these frenzied ceremonies vary not only in size and shape but in other ways too. Some show a face in profile, others in full view. Some are single-faced, others are double-faced (masks within masks); there are even masks with three, four, or five faces. The facial expressions are happy, fierce, terrifying, fearful, anguished, trancelike, or calm. They resemble humans, animals, or birds. Portrait masks are realistically carved to represent actual people. Secret society and crest masks represent animals and birds with human characteristics. Many have combined features, such as a human face with a bird's beak for a nose, or two sets of ears: human and animal. Others are stylized animal and bird masks. Transformation masks incorporate human, animal, *and* bird faces in any combination.

Facial features identify tribal preferences. The Tsimshian and Haida tribes used shapes that were clearly carved and life-size. The Kwakiutl and Bella Coola made features larger than life. Some masks are covered with paint and others have exposed raw wood. Mask carvers used red cedar bark templates to make features of equal size on opposite sides of a mask. Eye patterns are basically round and oval, with brows that are broad and rounded or angular. Eyes are a distinguishing feature of Northwest Coast masks.

HOW TO MAKE A NORTHWEST COAST INDIAN-STYLE MASK

Kwakiutl—Crest Blue-and-black face and fin, with red nostrils and lips. Round white frame with black-and-red designs.

Kwakiutl—Crest Green and white with red cheeks, mouth, and tongue. Mouth face is orange with green features. Top face is green and white, with red lips.

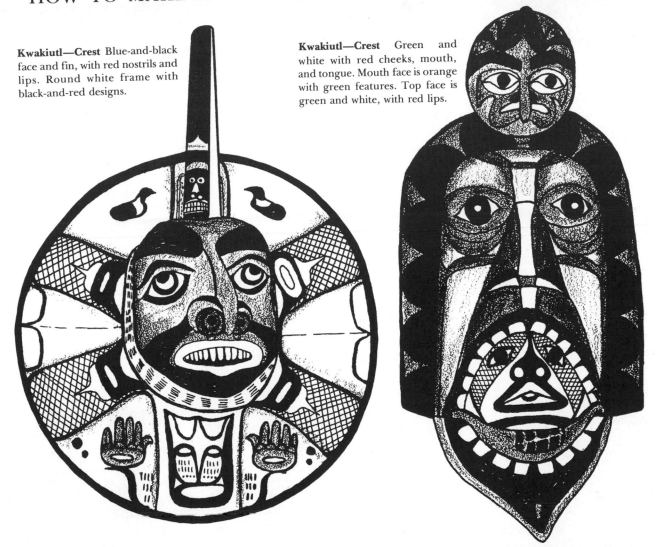

Small lightweight masks were held on the head by a strong cord attached at the back. Bulkier masks, with more weight, required a series of cords or belts made from hide. Large masks required webbing made from bent twigs that fitted over the head of the wearer. Very heavy large masks had a harness that fitted around the wearer's shoulders and across his chest.

It would be very difficult to carve and wear heavy wooden masks such as the Northwest Coast Indians wore. To make masks with the characteristics of those worn by these Indians, begin with the same basic techniques illustrated on pages 12 and 13 described for the Iroquois False Faces. Copy one of the masks shown in this chapter, or create one of your own.

Kwakiutl—Numal Blue with red designs.

Bella Bella Blue with purple-and-white designs. Red lips, ears, and nostrils.

Bella Coola—Moon Blue with black brows, red nostrils, lips and rim.

Kwakiutl—Hawk Spirit Green and white, with brown eyes and nostrils. Blue nose, red lips, and designs.

Tlingit Light blue with purple features and designs.

Tlingit—Bear Purple with red lips, nostrils, and ear designs. Black brows and eyes.

30

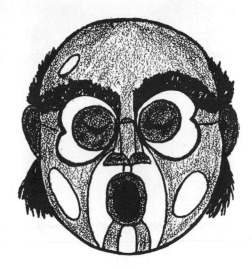

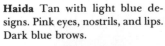

Kwakiutl Blue and white with red eyes, nostrils, ears and lips. Black brows and hair.

Haida Tan with light blue designs. Pink eyes, nostrils, and lips. Dark blue brows.

Kwakiutl—Sun Pink with black brows, red eyes, and nostrils. Blue nose and design. Blue-and-red rim.

Kwakiutl Black, white, red, and gray-green. Purple-and-white rim. Black, gray-green, and red surrounding shapes.

Salish—Mythical Being Black with white designs. Red around eyes, stripes, and beaks.

Tsimshian—Wind Spirit White with red nostrils and lips. Black brows and rim.

31

Kwakiutl double-face mask

DOUBLE-FACED MASKS (Mask within mask) Create one mask using any method used for the Iroquois False Faces. When dry, cover mask with plastic wrap, and use the same or any other method for a covering mask. When covering mask is dry, cut it in half vertically. Glue or staple felt hinges to the edges of both masks. Pull a string through holes in eyes, or elsewhere, to open and close the top mask.

Gauze applied over the balloon method (page 14) makes both masks at once.

EASY MASKS Use the same cardboard method described for Iroquois False Faces on page 15. Make a larger covering mask. Cut it in half vertically. Add tabs and attach to first mask with staples. If the covering mask is an animal or bird, make each side of the snout or beak separately.

EASIEST MASK Draw mask in three parts and fold sides to open and close.

Kwakiutl—Wolf Crest *Outer face,* blue with white around eyes, red nostrils and lips. Black eyes and brows. *Inner face,* natural wood with red designs, black eyes and brows.

Haida Natural wood with black designs.

Kwakiutl—Ogress Crest *Outer face,* black with red eyes and lips. Fur brows and moustache. *Inner face,* natural wood, black brows, eyes and moustache. Red lips.

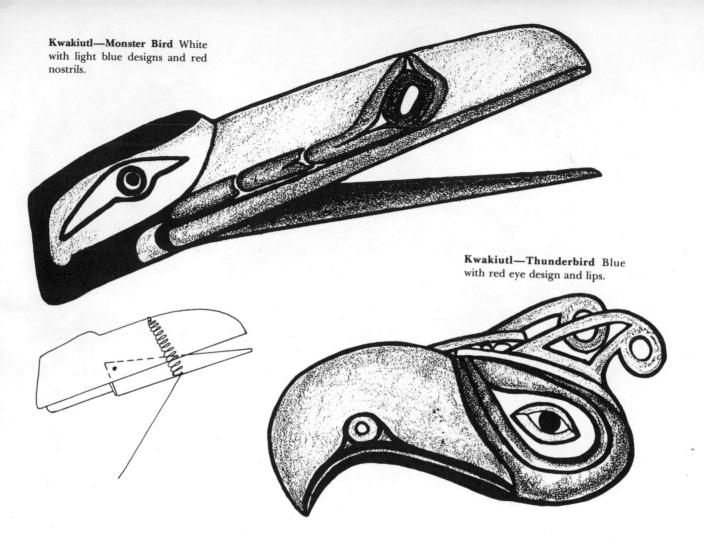

Kwakiutl—Monster Bird White with light blue designs and red nostrils.

Kwakiutl—Thunderbird Blue with red eye design and lips.

LARGE-SNOUT OR BEAKED MASKS

Layer papier-mâché strips over a frame. Make frames from rolled and taped newspapers, wire mesh, cardboard cartons, or corrugated cardboard. A piece of wire cut from a hanger becomes a hinge to attach the bottom of a beak or jaw and allows it to open. A spring inside the mouth will hold it closed, and a string underneath will pull it open.

ROLLING EYES To make rolling eyes, place two Ping-Pong balls on a piece of wire cut from a hanger. Paint black eyeballs, and attach a string with pins to the backs of each ball.

Tsimshian—Sea Monster Natural wood with blue designs and brows. Red nostrils and lips.

Kwakiutl—Wolf Blue with white around eyes, red nostrils, lips, and crown. White skull.

Nootka—Wolf Blue with red lips, designs, and crown.

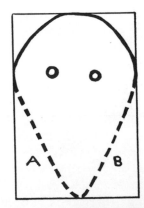

LARGE-FACE MASKS Draw and cut masks from cartons or corrugated cardboard. Glue or staple felt hinges.

EASY RAVEN MASKS (Or any beak or snout mask)
1. Copy pattern on paper 12 inches by 19 inches (22 cm., 310 cm.)
2. Cut solid lines. Fold broken lines.
3. Staple A to B. Draw and paint designs.

ALASKAN ESKIMO MASKS

Eskimos inhabit the arctic coasts of America from Greenland to Alaska, as well as a small part of the northern Asiatic coast. The Alaskan Eskimos, however, were more involved with mask making than Eskimos living in any of these other areas. These Indians made the most imaginative masks of all, ranging from realistic to fantastic. Some are small and cover only half the face. Others are large enough to cover the entire body. Most masks are carved of driftwood from spruce or cottonwood trees, and usually resemble a man, a beast, or a bird. Masks that represent a spirit being usually have one distorted feature.

The Eskimos believed that the world was filled with good and evil spirits that could make an appearance whenever they chose. Every animal, object, element, and place possessed spirits. Each person was believed to have many spirits within him. Spirits were so important to the Eskimos that their very lives depended upon how they treated them. The Eskimos observed many taboos, such as not saying certain words for fear of offending a spirit. Catastrophe and illness might result from such an offense.

The Eskimos depended upon shamans to communicate with the spirits. Almost every family had its own shaman, who diagnosed and cured the sick, guided hunters to find game, gave instructions to defeat an enemy, and forecast the weather. The people looked to their shamans for protection.

The shaman's mask was very important. It was always ugly and often had a big tooth sticking out of the mouth. It was splashed with alder-bark paint to represent dripping blood. The shaman usually made his own mask in the image of a guardian spirit about whom he had dreamed.

Other masks were made by skilled carvers who followed a shaman's directions, or who made masks in traditional designs. Shamans oversaw the making of all masks, which were always carved in secret.

Masks were worn in many dance festivals honoring the spirits of the animals and birds that were important for food. Because the Eskimos performed these dances to please the animal spirits, the masks had to be beautiful, and they were worn by the best dancers. Men generally wore face masks; women wore small masks on their fingers.

Every mask had its own story and dance. New masks, new songs, and new dance dramas were composed for every festival, although old ones were included. A new dance drama was performed first by the shaman who had created it or by someone who had learned it from him. The Eskimos rehearsed songs and dances many weeks before a festival. Sometimes a dancer used two different masks during the same dance. Although dance dramas portrayed numerous events of Eskimo life, they mainly concerned survival. Nothing was too trivial, whether it was hunting, fishing, fighting, picking ber-

Shamans often bang on a large tambourine-like instrument. Shaman's mask has a white face, gray-green shape around the eye, and reddish brown lips. Attachments are reddish brown, except for fish, which is white.

ries, or gathering bird eggs.

Festivals often lasted three or four days. The most important displays of masks were at the Messenger Feast and the Bladder Festival. The Messenger Feast was performed for hunters seeking to win favor from the animals they would hunt for food. The Bladder Festival was a memorial service for all the food animals that had been killed in the preceding year. The Eskimos believed that an animal's soul resided in its bladder.

Dancers wore humorous masks at certain festivals to which guests from another village were invited. The masked performers conducted a contest with the visitors to try to make them laugh. If they succeeded, the hosts could ask the visitors for anything they wanted.

The ceremonial house for festivals, called a *kazgi,* would be crowded with spectators. A cleared space at one end was reserved for the stage, and seal-oil lamps provided light. Singers and drummers created a rhythmic accompaniment to the dancing. A typical drama might begin with a dancer wearing a crow mask and swinging onto the stage by a rope from the roof. The chorus would announce the story of a hunter who failed to catch his prey. The dancer cawed and shrieked, talked and mumbled, playing the role of the crow. Then, changing to another mask, the dancer told how the crow had frightened away a deer with its terrible shrieks and how it had torn holes in the

37

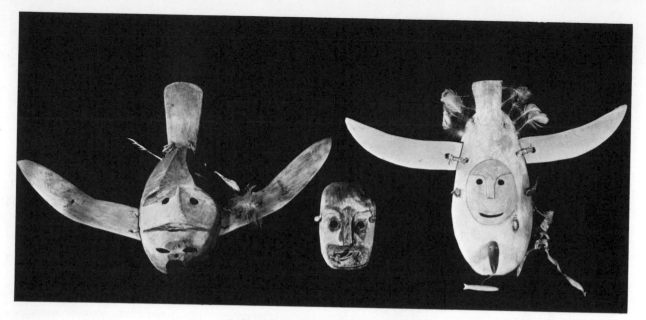

Left to right: Gull, Bad Dream, Crow.

hunter's fishing nets. The chorus sang softly in the background. The hunter pleaded with the spirit of the crow, and the crow spirit answered that this was the hunter's share of trouble. Throughout the drama, four women, wearing tiny masks on their fingers, flanked the dancer and waved their hands in rhythmic gestures.

Some dramas were solo dances, while others required many masked and unmasked performers. They varied in length and sometimes lasted more than two hours. Not only did these ceremonies provide the Eskimos with religious observance, entertainment, music, and art, but they also had a great social significance. They contributed to keeping peaceful relations within the village as well as with other tribes and other villages.

SHAPES, COLORS, AND FEATURES

Eskimo masks were either left unpainted or were painted with soft colors that did not detract from the shape of the masks. The artist applied natural pigments to the light-colored driftwood, using red and yellow from ocher and alder bark soaked in urine, blue from copper oxide, green from fungus, purple from swamp grass, black from ashes or graphite, and white from white clay. Many masks were painted with a white background. The Eskimos made masks in many shapes and sizes with any combination of eyes, nose, and mouth.

EYES Shapes for eyes were cut to enable the wearer to see. In rare cases, when eyes were not cut out, the wearer looked through the nostrils or the mouth. Eye

Left to right: Father of Mosquito, Crow, Messenger of the
Silver Salmon, Messenger of the Otter.

shapes are round, crescent-shaped, oval, teardrop, half-moon, almond, or slits.

NOSES Some are made with natural human shapes, slender or bulbous. Often spirit masks have no nose at all. Noses also appear in the shapes of a comma, triangle, crescent, circle, or any geometric shape, either singly or in pairs.

MOUTHS Shapes without lips are open or closed, down-curved, up-curved, slanting, skewed, round, or egglike. If a mouth has teeth, they are made of wood, bone, or ivory. Sometimes they are real animals' teeth (usually from a dog). Teeth are also painted onto a mask.

EARS Eskimo masks seldom have ears.

DECORATION AND ATTACHMENTS Mask makers used almost anything they could find for decoration, including feathers, porcupine quills, animal and human hair, fur, cotton, grass, bark, roots, rawhide, animal intestines, beads, string, crockery pieces, brass, copper, lead, iron, ivory, and wood. They often attached pieces of wood carved into various shapes. These attachments represent guardians, parts of the body, hunting devices, food, or any symbols related to the function of the mask.

HOW TO MAKE AN ALASKAN ESKIMO-STYLE MASK

Eskimo masks can be made using any of the methods described for Iroquois False Faces. A quicker method is to use corrugated cardboard. Copy any of the masks illustrated, or create your own. All sorts of cut-out shapes, feathers (real or paper), fur, hair, shells, and discarded small toys or parts can be attached for decoration. Although attachments usually have symbolic meaning, sometimes they were added for movement and sound. Try to be as imaginative as the Eskimos were.

EASY MASK Follow instructions using soaked cardboard as described on page 15 for Iroquois False Faces. Include attachments when drawing mask shape.

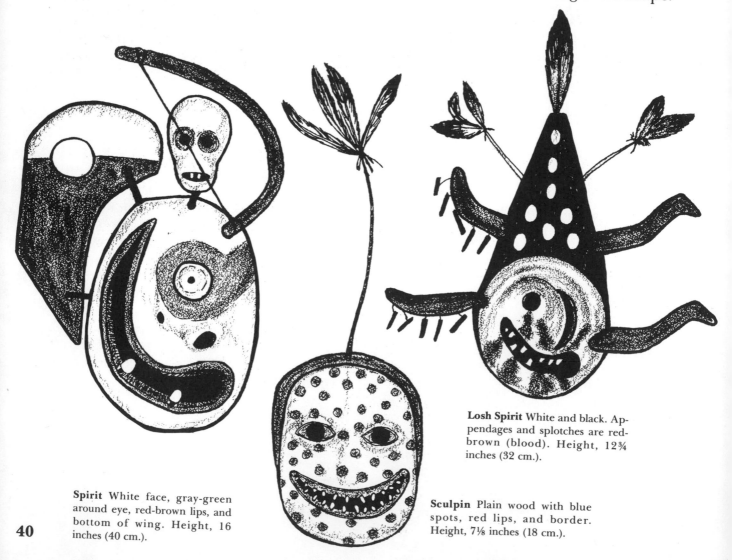

Spirit White face, gray-green around eye, red-brown lips, and bottom of wing. Height, 16 inches (40 cm.).

Losh Spirit White and black. Appendages and splotches are red-brown (blood). Height, 12¾ inches (32 cm.).

Sculpin Plain wood with blue spots, red lips, and border. Height, 7⅛ inches (18 cm.).

40

Guillemot Blue and white. Height, 9 inches (23 cm.).

Spirit Top white, bottom blue. Height, 11½ inches (29 cm.).

Crane Plain wood with red features. Height, 30 inches (76 cm.).

Ice Bubble White with red borders. Height, 8 inches (20 cm.).

Mythical Being Light red face with dark red splashes (blood). Height, 20 inches (50 cm.).

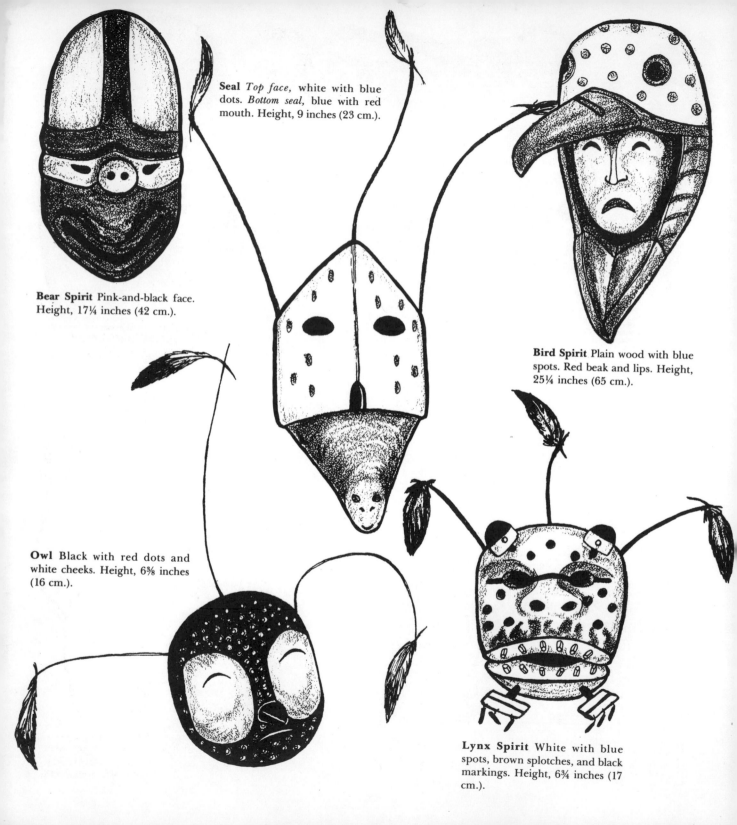

Seal *Top face,* white with blue dots. *Bottom seal,* blue with red mouth. Height, 9 inches (23 cm.).

Bear Spirit Pink-and-black face. Height, 17¼ inches (42 cm.).

Bird Spirit Plain wood with blue spots. Red beak and lips. Height, 25¼ inches (65 cm.).

Owl Black with red dots and white cheeks. Height, 6⅜ inches (16 cm.).

Lynx Spirit White with blue spots, brown splotches, and black markings. Height, 6¾ inches (17 cm.).

Being and Spirit White mask with doors. Black outlining red on arms and legs. Height, 11½ inches (29 cm.).

Sea Parrot *Outer face*, blue with white spots. *Inner face*, white. Height, 22 inches (56 cm.).

Loon *Bird*, blue with white spots. *Face*, red with white line. Height, 10½ inches (27 cm.).

Bubbles Rising White upper portion, blue lower portion. Red hands, white spots. Height, 20 inches (50 cm.).

Bad Spirit White with red eyes (white dots on left eye). Red mouth. Height, 6¾ inches (17 cm.).

Bird Gray and white. 2¾ inches × 3 inches (7 cm. × 7½ cm.).

Oval Face Black with red border. 4¾ inches × 2¾ inches (12 cm. × 7 cm.).

Star Plain wood. 5 inches × 2¾ inches (13 cm. × 7 cm.).

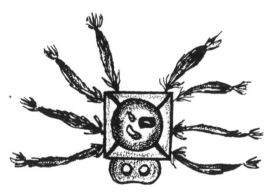

Long Face Blue and white. 5 inches × 1¾ inches (13 cm. × 4.5 cm.).

Square Face Plain wood. 4 inches × 2¾ inches (10 cm. × 7 cm.).

Round Face Plain wood. 3¼ inches × 3¼ inches (8.5 cm. × 8.5 cm.).

FINGER MASKS Finger masks were worn only by women. Their facial shapes are carved from ivory or wood to resemble people, animals, or birds. Some are geometric in form. Ranging from three to five inches long, they are usually painted and trimmed with feathers and caribou hair. Finger masks were originally worn in pairs and were held onto a finger by a ring, a wand, or a stem. Some of them duplicated the dancer's mask in miniture.

A finger mask can be made of papier-mâché. Make a copy of one illustrated, about three inches long from the top to the base of the ring. Shape the base by applying papier-mâché (see page 12) over folded and bent paper or wire. When dry, paint and trim with real or paper feathers and fanned-out absorbent cotton attached with white glue.

EASY FINGER MASKS Draw, color, cut, and add trimmings to a finger mask made of cardboard.

MORE MASKS

CHEROKEE The Cherokee Indians of North Carolina carved wooden masks similar to the Iroquois masks. Called *booger* masks, they were seldom painted, and their carving was less intricate. The Cherokees also made masks from large gourds.

Booger masks can be made using any of the methods for Iroquois False Faces. If you can find a large enough gourd, copy the mask shown. You will need smaller gourds for a nose and horns.

NASKAPI, NAVAHO, AND ZUNI The Naskapi Indians, an Algonquin tribe of the Northeast, made masks of animal hide, which they painted. Similar hide masks were also worn by Navaho and Zuni rain priests of the Southwest.

You can make masks resembling these hide faces by using tan felt and acrylic paints. Make the Zuni beard of red or black yarn, or unraveled and painted twine. Glue fake fur onto the Navaho mask.

APACHE The medicine men of the Apaches—another tribe of the Southwest—wore black cloth hood masks with large headdresses called *tabletas*. Like the Kachina masks, the Apache tabletas were made of yucca wood strips.

Cut and sew together a hood cut from a square piece of black felt, 15 inches by 15 inches (250 cm. square). The tableta can be made of cardboard with large tabs glued inside slits on the top of the hood. Tongue depressors or Popsicle sticks glued onto a strip of cardboard will make the tableta look more authentic. Paint tableta with poster or acrylic paints.

Cherokee

Naskapi

Zuni

Navaho

Apache

45

ZUNI SHALAKOS The Zuni carried Shalako masks on poles held above the head. They also wore skirts that covered the entire head and body.

Materials: grocery bag, papier-mâché paste and soaked newspaper strips, two long egg cartons, several cloth strips, paint, a small metal spring, string, rolling eyes (page 34), black crepe paper, cardboard horns, feathers, and ruff (page 25).

1. Stuff the grocery bag with newspapers, and coat the bag with three layers of newspaper strips dipped into paste.
2. To make a top beak, attach one egg-carton lid with dipped strips.
3. Attach another egg-carton lid with cloth strips dipped in paste to make the bottom half of the beak.
4. Attach the spring to the front ends of the top and bottom beaks.
5. Remove newspaper stuffing and make rolling eyes described for Northwest Coast masks. Place balls in cut-out eye holes, and insert wires through sides of mask.
6. Paint mask a bright color. Add fringed black crepe-paper hair, cardboard horns, and real or crepe-paper feathers.
7. Make a crepe-paper ruff as described for Kachina masks.

ASSINIBOIN An Assiniboin clown mask was made of canvas. These Indians lived primarily in the area bordering Lake Superior.

Make a mask of this type by sewing a seam 2 inches (5 cm.) in from the edge of an old pillowcase. Cut a fringe all around the edge. Paint it with poster paint. Canvas or felt can also be used. Be sure to leave an opening for your head, as shown.

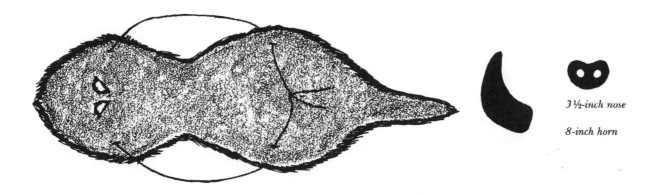

3½-inch nose

8-inch horn

PLAINS INDIANS The Plains Indians wore buffalo masks because they worshipped this animal. They also considered buffalo hides sacred.

1. Cut fake fur, 18 inches wide and 36 inches long (300 cm., 600 cm.) into the shape shown.
2. Knot and pull a string through a hole on each side, and tie underneath. Cut out eye holes.
3. Draw horns and nose on cardboard. Paint them black and cut them out. Glue them in place.

47

IROQUOIS BUSHY HEADS

IROQUOIS BUSHY HEADS Also known as Husk Faces, these masks are made of twilled or braided corn husks. They represent spirits of farmers believed to live on the other side of the earth. The masked messengers visited the Iroquois every year during a mid-winter festival.

Materials: paper plate, tan crepe paper, pencil, scissors, glue.

1. Using a paper plate, draw and cut holes for eyes and mouth.
2. Turn plate upside down. Glue a wad of paper under a crepe-paper nose.
3. Cut crepe paper in strips and braid into 12-inch lengths (30 cm.).
4. Coil and glue braids around holes and nose. Cover face with braids, leaving half an inch (1.3 cm.) around the edge.
5. Cut crepe-paper fringes and glue them around the edge of the mask.

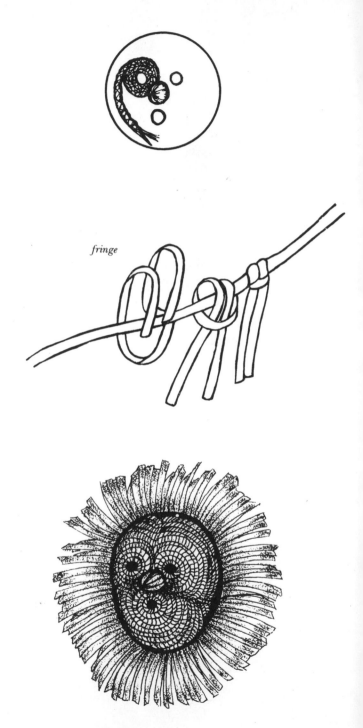

fringe